CANAL HOUSE
COOKING

CANAL HOUSE
No. 6 Coryell Street
Lambertville, NJ 08530
thecanalhouse.com

ISBN 978-0-9827394-0-2

Printed in China

Book design by CANAL HOUSE, a group of artists who collaborate on design projects.
This book was designed by Melissa Hamilton, Christopher Hirsheimer & Teresa Hopkins.
Edited by Margo True & Copyedited by Valerie Saint-Rossy.
Editorial assistance by Julie Sproesser

Distributed to the trade by
Andrews McMeel Publishing, LLC
an Andrews McMeel Universal company
1130 Walnut Street, Kansas City, Missouri 64106

www.andrewsmcmeel.com

11 12 13 14 OGP 10 9 8 7 6 5 4 3 2

ATTENTION: SCHOOLS AND BUSINESSES
Andrews McMeel books are available at quantity discounts with bulk purchase for
educational, business, or sales promotional use. For information, please e-mail
the Andrews McMeel Publishing Special Sales Department:
specialsales@amuniversal.com

CANAL HOUSE
COOKING

Volume Nº 4

Hamilton & Hirsheimer

Welcome to Canal House—our studio, workshop, dining room, office, kitchen, and atelier devoted to good ideas and good work relating to the world of food. We write, photograph, design, and paint, but in our hearts we both think of ourselves as cooks first.

Our loft studio is in an old red brick warehouse. A beautiful lazy canal runs alongside the building. We have a simple galley kitchen. Two small apartment-size stoves sit snugly side by side against a white tiled wall. We have a dishwasher, but prefer to hand wash the dishes so we can look out of the tall window next to the sink and see the ducks swimming in the canal or watch the raindrops splashing into the water.

And every day we cook. Starting in the morning we tell each other what we made for dinner the night before. Midday, we stop our work, set the table simply with paper napkins, and have lunch. We cook seasonally because that's what makes sense. So it came naturally to write down what we cook. The recipes in our books are what we make for ourselves and our families all year long. If you cook your way through a few, you'll see that who we are comes right through in the pages: that we are crazy for tomatoes in summer, make braises and stews all fall, and turn oranges into marmalade in winter.

Canal House Cooking is home cooking by home cooks for home cooks. We use ingredients found in most markets. All the recipes are easy to prepare for the novice and experienced cook alike. We want to share them with you as fellow cooks along with our love of food and all its rituals. The everyday practice of simple cooking and the enjoyment of eating are two of the greatest pleasures in life.

CHRISTOPHER HIRSHEIMER served as food and design editor for *Metropolitan Home* magazine, and was one of the founders of *Saveur* magazine, where she was executive editor. She is a writer and a photographer.

MELISSA HAMILTON cofounded the restaurant Hamilton's Grill Room in Lambertville, New Jersey, where she served as executive chef. She worked at *Martha Stewart Living*, *Cook's Illustrated*, and at *Saveur* as the food editor.

Christopher and Melissa in the Canal House kitchen

It's Always Five O'Clock Somewhere
the arturo 8, juicy fruit cocktail 8, lemon cordial 8
dark & stormy 11, barley water 11

Working up an Appetite
frico 14, shrimp ceviche 17, halibut with tomato, mint, and lemon 17
quick-cured salmon 17, jamón serrano on toast with red tomato preserves 18
little blue reds 21, hot sausages & cold oysters 21

Avocado Love
in praise of the hass avocado 25, an avocado with crab salad 25
cold avocado & cucumber soup 26
guacamole and chips 29, chicken tacos for lunch 32
avocado, arugula, and grapefruit salad 33

A Big Bowl of Soup
chilled cauliflower soup 36, consommé bellevue 37
tomato-cucumber water 38, corn soup with lobster and avocado 39

Fines Herbes
green sauce 42, toasted bread crumbs 42
summer mayonnaise 43, omelet with fines herbes 44
pasta with parsley and toasted walnut sauce 47
parsley-potato salad 48

Luncheon Salads
salmon salad 52, halibut salad 52, canal house curried chicken salad 53
shrimp salad 53, chopped ham salad with hard-boiled eggs 54
anytime egg salad 54

Farm Stands, Roadside Tables & the Garden

ALL SUMMER LONG, LITTLE FARMERS' MARKETS pop up like wildflowers around our county—happily, they seem to be spreading. It might be Thursday afternoon in the high school parking lot or Sunday morning in a field next to an old barn. One of our favorites, the Ottsville Farmers' Market, goes from Friday afternoon until sunset. It's on a beautiful old farm, Linden Hill Gardens, that has blossomed into a nursery for rare plants. A local band jams as the farmers set up in the gravel courtyard next to the old farmhouse and its *potager*. Lush flowering shrubs and trees are everywhere, surrounding you with the loveliness of summer.

In the center of the courtyard is a fire pit and a primitive outdoor kitchen. Something is always cooking, and sometimes there's a little wine to taste. A farmer who raises pork and poultry hangs up posters in his tent showing his farm and how he raises his animals. He sells the fat, spicy pork sausages that we love. Two men who sell seafood arrive with all their fish packed in tubs of ice. A straw-hatted young farmer fills up his stand's big baskets with snow-white heads of cauliflower, bright green lettuces, dirty carrots, and hard little freshly dug potatoes. We want to buy everything. When the market is in full swing, someone comes up with a brilliant idea for the fire pit—sausages and oysters. The pork and poultry man cooks little porkies on the grill and the fish guys start shucking. We buy one of each and take a bite of hot sausage bursting with smoky juices, then slurp down an ice-cold briny oyster. We get back in line for more. Farmers and shoppers, little kids, even a dog or two stand around the grill, eating out of hand, everyone is talking at once about how delicious this all is—a great summer experience.

One of our favorite pastimes is to drive around the countryside looking for roadside tables. Twelve years ago we came across an elderly gentleman patiently sitting by a small stand in front of his modest house. There on his table were quart baskets filled with jewel-like red currants. He also had some strawberries and small zucchini lying on the table. But the currants were the prize. They grow in delicate clusters and need to be picked with care, and yet he was selling quarts of the berries for 2.50 each. Clearly money wasn't his motivation. The gentleman had planted his bushes years ago and you could sense his pride when we complimented him on the fruit. We made jars and jars of gorgeous red currant jelly with his fruit, and we always saved a few to give him on the next visit. He would smile and gracefully accept them. Every year we'd hold our breaths as we rounded the curve in the road just before his stand. Would he be there? For a long time, he was. Then one year the stand was empty. Who would pick the berries? Early this summer, we noticed new curtains hanging in the windows—someone bought the house. A small table has appeared out front again with a few boxes of currants and a cardboard honor box. And so the beat goes on.

We both plant home gardens every year. Even at Canal House, where we have only a narrow balcony just outside the windows, we fill pots and boxes with herbs, tomatoes, cucumbers, and even strawberries. We love our gardens. We tend them and fuss over them, and they give us back so much. Each day we cook what we harvest—a handful of young green beans, a bouquet of chard—responding to whatever our vegetable patches have to offer. We realize that our gardens are far more than the vegetables they give us.

The way we cook in the summer couldn't be simpler. In fact, we call ourselves salt-and-pepper cooks. We forsake the convenience of the supermarket and live in the season—slicing big ripe tomatoes, preserving tomatoes, grilling leeks, roasting chickens and slathering them with herb butter, foraging for chanterelles, turning corn into succotash, baking berry cobblers, and making apricot jam. Cooking is a wonderful way to immerse yourself in the season around you. Now get out there and cook.

Christopher & Melissa

it's always five o'clock somewhere

THE ARTURO

A friend and Canal House supporter sent us this recipe to help us meet our publishing deadline. And it did. We pass it on for you to share with your friends, too. Adjust the sweetness to suit your taste.

Pour 1 tablespoon real maple syrup and the juice of a hand-squeezed, fat, thin-skinned lime into a glass. Add 2 ounces Mount Gay Eclipse rum and stir to mix. Fill the glass with cracked ice then float Zaya Gran Reserva rum or Rhum Barbancourt (15 year) on top. ——*makes 1*

JUICY FRUIT COCKTAIL

We love the velvety taste of Trinidad's 10 Cane rum, made with fermented sugar cane juice, not molasses like most rums. Or for a clean summery flavor, try an artisanal Brazilian cachaça.

Fill a glass with ice, add 2 ounces white rum or cachaça, then pour in passion fruit or guava juice. Depending on the size of your glass, you may have to tinker and taste a bit to get the ratio of rum to fruit juice right. Give half a fat thin-skinned lime a good squeeze over the glass, then toss it into the drink.——*makes 1*

LEMON CORDIAL
makes 1 quart

Mix this intensely flavored cordial with flat or fizzy water. We like to muddle fresh mint or lemon verbena in the glass first.

6 whole lemons, washed   ⅔ cup granulated sugar

Using a vegetable peeler, remove the rind from 3 of the lemons and put into a mixing bowl. Juice all the lemons and add to the bowl. Add the sugar to the bowl. Pour in 2½ cups boiling water. Stir until all of the sugar has dissolved. Set aside and allow to cool and steep for 12 hours in the refrigerator.

DARK & STORMY

We've been on a dark and stormy jag that started late in the spring. Every evening when cocktail hour rolls around and the mercury reaches up into hot, we start to salivate for the cooling effects of this drink (left).

Put a big handful of ice cubes into a tall glass. Pour 1½–2 ounces dark rum over the rocks. Top it off with ginger beer (about 4 ounces). Add the juice of 1 lemon wedge and 1 lime wedge, garnishing the drink with the wedge of lime —— *makes 1*

BARLEY WATER (THE QUEEN'S RECIPE)
makes about 1 quart

This is Mum's recipe for barley water. If memory serves, it was originally called the Queen's Barley Water, pulled from a newspaper, the original now lost in time. Refreshing, nourishing, and very good for your skin, Mum kept a jug of this in the fridge to minister her little clucks, effectively, and most delicious it was, too. —— *Jeremy Lee, chef of Blue Print Café, London*

Jeremy grew up in Scotland's beautiful Taye River Valley, very near Balmoral, the royal summer retreat, where there is an ancient tradition of drinking barley water for its restorative attributes. Fifty years ago, popular lore credited the young Queen Elizabeth's beautiful complexion to barley water—take that, Botox!

1 cup pearl barley	2 lemons
6 oranges	Demarara sugar to taste

Wash the barley well. Tip it into a pot and cover with 8 cups water. Bring to a boil over medium-high heat. Reduce the heat to low and gently simmer for an hour. Strain and reserve the barley for another use (it is excellent in a soup of sorts), and pour the barley water into a large jug or pitcher. Add in the rind of 3 of the oranges and 1 of the lemons, and all the juice from the oranges and lemons. Stir in sugar to taste—it should not be too sweet! Refrigerate until cool and drink within a day or two.

working up an appetite

FRICO

These little lacy cheese crisps—as thin as tissue paper and as brittle as a shot nerve—are a traditional Friulian farmhouse snack. Since Americans love anything "salty and crispy", it's no wonder they are now served across the country. But the most memorable frico I ever had was as big as a dinner plate.

One summer my sister, her two little boys, and my daughter and I were staying in Italy about as far south as you can go, at the bottom tip of the heel, in the small port town of Santa Maria di Léuca. It had been a long scorching day with no escape from the heat. Finally twilight came and with it stars began to glow, lights twinkled on the little boats bobbing in the harbor, a breeze blew up, and our moods lifted. My sister quietly slipped off to the kitchen and came back out moments later carrying two icy cold Negronis and one big frico. As we sat on the terrace overlooking the water, drinking our drinks and breaking off pieces of the delicate frico, I instantly knew that *that* moment and those flavors would be deliciously inextricable. ——MH

For each frico, you'll need about 1 cup freshly grated parmigiano-reggiano or other hard Italian grating cheese. Heat a large nonstick skillet over medium heat. Sprinkle the cheese into the skillet, in a round, thin layer, with ragged edges. Toast the cheese until it gets lacy as it begins to melt together and to turn deep golden brown, 1–2 minutes. Lift up an edge of the cheese with a thin spatula, then gradually slide it under and carefully turn the frico over. This takes a little practice so don't worry if the frico bunches up a bit; it adds character. Toast the second side until it is golden, even a little darker if you like, then transfer it to a plate. Frico can be shaped while still warm and pliable. They will be crisp when cool. Make as many as you like, but make them the same day you plan to eat them so they stay crisp. ——*makes 1 big frico*

As you prepare these simple ceviches and the cured salmon, remember to use only the freshest seafood and keep everything as cold as possible. Fat, juicy, thin-skinned limes will yield the most juice. Kosher salt is good for curing (it dissolves quickly) but try Maldon or an Irish or French *fleur de sel* for finishing the dish.

SHRIMP CEVICHE

Toss 1 pound halved, deveined, peeled, medium, raw shrimp together with the juice of 5–6 fat thin-skinned limes and a big pinch of kosher salt in a bowl. Cover with plastic wrap and refrigerate for 1 hour. Just before serving, drain the shrimp and discard the lime juice. Add 2 finely chopped scallions, 2 tablespoons minced chives, and 2 tablespoons cilantro leaves and toss everything together. Serve very cold on chilled plates with sliced avocado or grapefruit supremes and a sprinkle of *fleur de sel.* — *serves 4*

HALIBUT WITH TOMATOES, MINT, AND LEMON

Cut a 1-pound halibut filet into 2 pieces. Wrap in plastic and freeze for 1–2 hours, until firm but not completely frozen. Remove from the freezer and thinly slice. Put the halibut slices into a bowl with the juice of 5–6 fat thin-skinned limes and a big pinch of kosher salt. Cover with plastic wrap and refrigerate for 1 hour. Just before serving, drain the halibut and discard the lime juice. Arrange the cold halibut on a chilled platter. Garnish with a chiffonade of fresh mint, minced lemon rind, diced peeled tomato, a sprinkle of red pepper flakes and a sprinkle of *fleur de sel.* — *serves 4*

QUICK-CURED SALMON

Thinly slice a 1-pound wild salmon filet diagonally into large, thin slices. Generously sprinkle Maldon salt or another flaky sea salt, and ground pepper onto a large platter. Arrange the salmon slices in a single layer on top of the salt and pepper, then sprinkle again with salt and pepper. Scatter with chopped dill leaves. Cover with plastic wrap, pressing it directly onto the salmon, and refrigerate for 2 hours. Remove the plastic wrap, drizzle with a really good extra-virgin olive oil, and scatter with sliced scallions and a handful of tiny celery leaves. Serve with thinly sliced, buttered pumpernickel or other good dark bread. — *serves 4*

JAMÓN SERRANO ON TOAST WITH RED TOMATO PRESERVES
makes as many as you want to make

There's a local store we frequent that's been carrying a nice selection of cured meats including the Spanish beauty, *jamón serrano*. We regard this ham with nearly the same respect the Spaniards do and serve it sliced—just thicker than prosciutto—with especially delicious things like a perfectly ripe avocado or with our sweet plump Red Tomato Preserves (page 64).

These toasts are so good we eat them for breakfast in the morning with *cafe con leche*. And then again at the end of the day with a glass of dry white wine or really cold *fino* sherry.

Brush small, thin slices of crusty bread with some really good olive oil and toast them in a preheated 400° oven until golden on each side. Let the toasts cool. Drape each toast with a slice (or half a slice if a whole one is too much) of serrano ham. Top the toasts with small spoonfuls of Red Tomato Preserves.

VARIATION: Serve thin slices of Manchego cheese on toasts topped with a small spoonful of Red Tomato Preserves.

LITTLE BLUE REDS
makes enough to fill 2 dozen tomato halves (about ¾ cup mash)

This blue cheese and butter mash is delicious against the sweetness of little cherry tomatoes and we serve them together as an hors d'oeuvre. It also makes for a nice breakfast slathered on warm toast (add to that combo a juicy summer peach and you've got yourself a little taste of heaven).

Mash together ¼ pound good blue cheese and 4 tablespoons softened salted butter in a small bowl. Season with coarsely ground black pepper. Spread on halved cherry tomatoes and garnish with chopped fresh parsley.

HOT SAUSAGES & COLD OYSTERS
make as many as you like

This is really just a suggestion of an amazing combination of flavor, texture, and temperature. You choose the type of sausage, from highly seasoned little porkies to spicy chorizo and everything in between. The variety of oysters will depend on what is the very freshest. Make sure that the oysters are ice-cold—they are less resistant and easier to open. If you don't know how to shuck oysters, be sure to befriend and invite someone who can pop them open without spilling any of their briny juice.

To grill the sausages, prepare a medium-hot hardwood, charcoal, or gas grill. Grill the sausages over the hottest part of the grill, turning them as they brown. When browned all over, move them to a cooler spot on the grill to finish cooking, turning them occasionally until they have cooked through. The grilling time will vary depending on your grill and the heat.

Serve the hot sausages and cold shucked oysters together, eating this treat like this: take a bite of hot juicy sausage, then chase it by slurping down an ice-cold oyster.

avocado love

Birthday Lunch

avocado with Singer olive oil and lemon
and jamón serrano

✤

big fat asparagus with a poached egg
and shaved parmesan

✤

strawberries with cassis
and soft-whipped cream

✤

A. Margaine
champagne, brut cuvée traditionnelle, NV

Melissa made a celebratory birthday lunch for Christopher at Canal House

IN PRAISE OF THE HASS AVOCADO

We have a friend who lives on a property in California with a garden full of Hass avocado trees. A couple times a year he packs up one of those large United States Postal Service flat-rate mailing boxes—If It Fits, It Ships— with as many avocados as he can safely fit and sends it off to us. They arrive in pristine condition, their pebbly skin dark green, not yet fully black, and the avocados themselves hard, not quite ripe. It is an incredible gift. We set them out to finish ripening in the studio, checking them each day to see if the flesh has begun to yield under the gentle pressure of our thumbs. We feel like avocado affineurs, coaxing the fruits to ripe perfection. Within a few days they're ready—outside their skin has blackened, inside their flesh is firm but softer now with a rich, creamy, buttery flavor.

And so we begin, we eat one after another. Breakfast, coarsely mashed on hot buttered toast, with a squeeze of lime, and a sprinkle of crunchy salt. Lunch, two halves filled with especially good olive oil, a big squeeze of lemon juice, salt, and cracked black pepper. Dinner, stuffed into a hot corn tortilla with lime juice, salt, and lots of chopped fresh cilantro. Couldn't be simpler, couldn't be more delicious.

AN AVOCADO WITH CRAB SALAD
serves 2

The sweet, smooth flavor and texture of a Hass avocado (and the convenient crater left in each half when pitted) make it the perfect partner for cold seafood salads like this ultra-simply dressed one made with crabmeat. The avocado "cup" that holds the salad will sit steady on the plate if you nick a little flat spot off the bottom of each peeled half.

½ pound Dungeness or jumbo
  lump crabmeat
3–4 tablespoons mayonnaise
4–6 tablespoons fresh lemon juice

Salt and pepper
Handful fresh parsley leaves,
  chopped
1 ripe Hass avocado

Gently mix together the crabmeat, mayonnaise, and lemon juice in a medium

continued

bowl. Season the crab salad with a little salt, if you like, and with some pepper. Fold in the parsley.

Just before serving, slice the avocado in half lengthwise, then twist the two halves in opposite directions to loosen the flesh from the pit. Pull the halves apart. Thwack the pit with the sharp side of the knife so that the blade lodges in the pit. Twist the knife, and the pit will lift out of the avocado. Peel off the skin and nick a little off the bottom of each half to keep the avocados steady on the plate. Spoon the crab salad into each avocado.

COLD AVOCADO & CUCUMBER SOUP

The recipe for this velvety cold soup is a hand-me-down, passed along to my mother from a neighbor friend, then on to me. The impulse to share a good thing—it's always like this with delicious, simple recipes. And now it's our turn to pass this keeper on to you. ——MH

Working in two batches to avoid overcrowding the blender, put 3 ripe, unblemished, pitted, and peeled Hass avocados, 1 cut-up unpeeled cucumber, 2 cloves garlic, 3 tablespoons fresh lemon juice, and 4 cups chicken stock into a blender and purée until smooth. Season with salt. Refrigerate the soup until it is well chilled. Serve it in pretty glasses or chilled bowls garnished with a dollop of sour cream and a dash of hot pepper sauce. We suggest you make this soup the same day you plan to serve it so it retains its pretty, pale green color. ——*serves 4*

GUACAMOLE AND CHIPS
serves 4–6 (or one)

This is the simplest of guacamoles and relies on ripe, unblemished Hass avocados. We have the best luck finding these beauties at our local Mexican grocery store. And it makes all the difference in the world if you fry your own chips. They taste like tortilla chips should taste and have a sturdiness just right for scooping up the chunky guacamole.

FOR THE CHIPS
Vegetable oil
12 corn tortillas
Salt

FOR THE GUACAMOLE
1–2 cloves garlic
Salt
6–8 ripe Hass avocados, halved and pitted
2–3 juicy thin-skinned limes, halved
½ bunch fresh cilantro, chopped

For the chips, add enough oil to a heavy skillet or wok to reach a depth of 2 inches. Heat the oil until it is hot but not smoking, ideally to a temperature of 350° (use a candy thermometer to check the temperature). Meanwhile, cut the tortillas into quarters.

Slip the tortillas, a few at a time, into the hot oil and fry them until golden and crisp, 1–2 minutes. Using a slotted spatula, transfer the chips as they're done to paper towels to drain. Season them with salt while still hot.

For the guacamole, use a pestle or wooden spoon to mash the garlic with a good pinch of salt in the bottom of a medium bowl. Scoop the avocado flesh into the bowl using a spoon or rubber spatula. Mash the avocados until chunky smooth. Squeeze the juice from some of the limes into the bowl, season with a little more salt, and mix well. Taste the guacamole and adjust the seasonings with more lime juice and/or salt. Stir in the cilantro. Serve the guacamole with the chips.

CHICKEN TACOS FOR LUNCH
serves 6

Our taco meals vary depending on what is on hand or left over. We often grill a chicken the night before while the grill is fired up for dinner, then serve it for taco lunch the next day. Tortillas taste best when they are hot off the fire, so one of us mans the stove, toasting the tortillas, as our family and guests assemble their tacos.

1 grilled or roasted whole chicken, at room temperature

Salt

2 seeded, peeled, and roasted poblano chiles

2 tablespoons extra-virgin olive oil

4–6 limes, cut into wedges

4–6 ripe Hass avocados, pitted, thickly sliced, and peeled

8 ounces grated queso Oaxaca or other semisoft grating cheese

1 cup Mexican *crema,* or sour cream thinned with heavy cream

6 scallions, chopped

½ bunch fresh cilantro

18–24 fresh corn tortillas

Pull the meat off the chicken and tear it into "nice"-size shreds, discarding the skin and bones. Put the meat in a serving dish and season it with salt.

Slice the poblano chiles into strips, put them in a serving dish, drizzle them with some of the olive oil, and season with salt.

Put the remaining ingredients, except for the tortillas, into individual serving dishes and bowls, squeezing some lime juice over the avocados to keep them from turning brown.

If you have a gas stovetop, warm the tortillas, one at a time, directly over a medium flame, toasting them on each side until warm and lightly flecked with char marks. Otherwise, heat a cast-iron skillet over medium heat. Add the tortillas one at a time, warming them until lightly toasted on each side. Stack the warm tortillas as they are done in a clean dishcloth, covering them up to keep them warm.

continued

To serve, put the chicken, hot tortillas, and all the accompaniments on the table so everyone can make their own tacos. We fill ours like this: scatter a little grated cheese on a warm tortilla, add a few pieces of chicken, some roasted chiles, a couple slices of avocado, a spoonful of *crema*, some scallions, and a sprig or two of cilantro. Squeeze some lime juice over everything, wrap the tortilla around the filling, and eat out of hand. It's a little messy but really delicious.

AVOCADO, ARUGULA, AND GRAPEFRUIT SALAD
serves 2–4

Avocado and grapefruit are clearly not the kind of fruits that grow in our backyards here in the Northeast, but this classic combination, with the addition of peppery arugula and radishes (that we gather right out of our own garden), tastes like a summer salad wherever you happen to be.

2 grapefruit, preferably Ruby Red
Juice of ½ lemon
2–3 tablespoons fruity olive oil
Salt and pepper

4 radishes, thinly sliced
2 big handfuls small arugula leaves
2 ripe Hass avocados, halved, pitted, thickly sliced, and peeled

Working with one grapefruit at a time, slice the ends off the fruit. Set the grapefruit on one of the cut ends and slice off the rind and white pith, exposing the flesh. Working over a bowl, cut along both sides of each segment to release it from the membrane, letting it drop into the bowl. (Since we really want to use just the grapefruit segments for this salad and not so much the juice, we don't squeeze out any extra juice from the spent fruit into the bowl. You may want to squeeze out the extra juice to drink.)

Add the lemon juice and olive oil to the bowl with the grapefruit segments. Season with salt and pepper. Add the radishes.

Divide the arugula and the avocados between 2–4 salad plates. Spoon some of the grapefruit and radishes on each. Dress each salad with some of the vinaigrette (there may be more vinaigrette than you need depending on how juicy the grapefruit are).

a big bowl of soup

CHILLED CAULIFLOWER SOUP
serves 6–8

We'll add a potato to some puréed vegetable soups to round out the flavor and give a silky mouthfeel, but the majestic cauliflower produces a creaminess on its own. We serve this simple, elegant soup cold—it's a pretty starter to a summer meal—but it can be served warm, if you prefer.

4 tablespoons butter
2 medium onions, chopped
1 celery rib, chopped
1 cauliflower, cored
6 cups chicken stock

Salt
Pinch of freshly grated nutmeg
2 cups heavy cream
Fresh chervil or chives

Melt the butter in a large pot over medium-low heat. Add the onions and celery, cover the pot, and sweat the vegetables until translucent, about 10 minutes.

Break the cauliflower into florets and add them to the pot. Pour in the stock and add 2 generous pinches of salt. Increase the heat to medium and gently boil the soup until the cauliflower is soft, 20–30 minutes. Add the nutmeg.

Let the soup cool, then purée it in batches in a blender or food processor. Strain the soup through a fine-mesh sieve into a bowl. Season with salt. Cover and refrigerate the soup until well chilled. It will keep, refrigerated, for up to 2 days.

Whisk the cream until soft peaks form. Serve the soup cold in chilled soup bowls, each garnished with a dollop of whipped cream and a sprig of chervil or a scattering of finely chopped chives.

Overleaf: left, Chilled Cauliflower Soup; right, Consommé Bellevue

CONSOMMÉ BELLEVUE
serves 2–4

This forgotten classic, always made with clear chicken and clam broth, tastes very modern—like a deconstructed New England clam chowder—and looks very elegant.

2 cups flavorful clam broth
2 cups flavorful chicken broth
Salt

¼–⅓ cup heavy cream
Small handful fresh chives

Gently bring the clam and chicken broths to a simmer over medium-low heat. Season to taste with a little salt.

Whisk the cream in a bowl until soft peaks form. Put a spoonful of the whipped cream on top of each serving, and garnish with lots of finely snipped chives.

TOMATO-CUCUMBER WATER
makes about 8 cups

This is hardly a recipe! But this beautifully flavored elixir is well worth the trouble. If you are making the aspic variation, use the ratio of 1 packet gelatin to 3 cups tomato-cucumber water. It will be soft and delicate, cool and refreshing with the flavor of an ethereal gazpacho.

4 pounds tomatoes, stemmed, cored, and quartered

1 large English cucumber, peeled and cut into large pieces

2 tablespoons salt

Finely minced chives

Finely minced fresh or preserved lemon rind

Purée the tomatoes and cucumbers with the salt in a food processor. Line a large bowl with a large piece of cheesecloth or a very thin, clean muslin kitchen towel. Pour the puréed tomatoes and cucumbers into the towel-lined bowl. Gather the ends of the towel and tie them into knots. Slip a long-handled wooden spoon or dowel through and under the knots and suspend the towel over the bowl so the tomato-cucumber water can slowly drip into the bowl. Resist the urge to squeeze the pulp in the towel, it will make the tomato-cucumber water cloudy. Allow the tomatoes to drip for 4–8 hours, then discard the pulp and refrigerate the tomato-cucumber water. Serve cold in chilled bowls or glasses with the chives and lemon rind.

VARIATION: To make Tomato-Cucumber Water Aspic, soften 1 packet unflavored gelatin in 2 tablespoons cool water in a medium bowl. Add ½ cup hot tomato-cucumber water and stir until the gelatin has dissolved. Stir in 2½ cups of cool tomato-cucumber water. Cover and refrigerate until it sets. It will be a soft gelatin. Spoon into chilled glasses or bowls and serve garnished with minced chives and lemon rind, and the chopped flesh of a seeded, peeled, ripe tomato.——*makes 3 cups*

CORN SOUP WITH LOBSTER AND AVOCADO
serves 4

In midsummer, corn is so tender, juicy, and sweet and the cobs so large and full that you may need to use fewer ears of corn. You can adjust the amounts of milk and corn to your liking. Most fish stores will be happy to save you the hassle and steam the lobster for you.

8 ears corn, shucked
6 cups whole milk
½ teaspoon red pepper flakes
Salt and pepper
Meat from one cooked lobster,
  cut into large pieces

2 Hass avocados, pitted, peeled,
  and cubed
1 thin-skinned lime, quartered
Chopped fresh cilantro

Cut the corn kernels off the cobs into a large pot, scraping the cobs to release all the milky juice. Break each cob in two or three pieces. Put all the cobs into the pot along with the milk. Add red pepper flakes and season with salt and pepper. Bring to a simmer over medium heat. Adjust the heat to maintain a very low simmer, cover, and cook for 30 minutes.

Using tongs, remove and discard the cobs. Purée the soup in a food processor, then strain it through a fine-mesh sieve into a bowl. Rinse out the pot then pour the puréed soup back in the pot. Taste, season with salt and pepper, then refrigerate the soup until cold.

Pour the soup into individual chilled bowls. Garnish, dividing the lobster and avocado cubes between the bowls. Serve with a squeeze of lime and lots of chopped cilantro.

fines herbes

GREEN SAUCE
makes about 1½ cups

Every culture has its version of this sauce. Some add chopped hard-boiled eggs, or vinegar, some hand-chop it for a more rustic texture. We serve it with grilled meat and fish, and even spoon it into mayonnaise.

1 cup pitted meaty green olives, such as Castelvetrano
1 cup packed fresh parsley leaves
1 cup packed basil leaves
1 clove garlic

6 anchovy filets
Juice and rind of ½ lemon
1 cup (more or less) really good extra-virgin olive oil

Put the olives, parsley, basil, garlic, anchovies, and lemon juice and rind in the bowl of a food processor. Purée, drizzling in the oil slowly. Transfer to a bowl and add a thin layer of olive oil to keep the sauce from turning dark.

TOASTED BREAD CRUMBS
(with lots of parsley and a little thyme)
makes 2 cups

We've gone on about the virtues of bread crumbs before—they are a staple in our everyday cooking. In the summer, when fresh herbs are so abundant, we add lots of them to these crunchy crumbs. We sprinkle them on everything from roasted tomatoes and stewy vegetables to pastas and shellfish.

2 cups coarse, fresh bread crumbs made from day-old bread
2 cloves garlic, finely chopped
⅓ cup extra-virgin olive oil
Salt and pepper

Leaves of 1 bunch fresh parsley, chopped
Leaves of 1 branch fresh thyme, chopped

Preheat the oven to 375°. Toss the bread crumbs, garlic, olive oil, and lots of salt and pepper together in a bowl, then spread the seasoned crumbs out in a shallow baking pan. Toast the crumbs until they are deep golden brown, 10–15 minutes. Remove the bread crumbs from the oven and let them cool completely, then stir in the parsley and thyme.

SUMMER MAYONNAISE
makes 2 cups

With all the delicious cold food there is to eat during the summer, you
need an equally delicious cold sauce to go with it. Of course, that would be
mayonnaise, and we make one with lots of fresh herbs and lighten it with
a good hit of lemon juice. We keep a small tub in the fridge and use it on
practically everything.

2 large egg yolks
½ clove garlic, minced
Salt
Juice of 2 lemons
1 cup canola oil

1 cup good, smooth, "buttery"
  olive oil
2 cups fresh, tender leaf herbs such
  as a mixture of parsley, tarragon, chives, chervil, and/or dill,
  chopped

Whisk together the egg yolks, garlic, pinch of salt, and about 2 tablespoons
of the lemon juice in a medium bowl. Combine the oils in a measuring cup
with a spout. Whisking constantly, add the oil to the yolks about 1 teaspoon
at a time. The sauce will thicken and emulsify. After you have added about
¼ cup of the oil, you can begin to slowly drizzle in the remaining oil as you
continue to whisk, until you have thick, glossy mayonnaise. Season with salt
and thin with as much of the remaining lemon juice as suits your taste. Stir
in the chopped herbs. Transfer the mayonnaise to a container. It will keep,
covered, in the refrigerator for up to 5 days.

OMELET WITH FINES HERBES
serves 1

A simple herb omelet accompanied by a leafy green salad or plate of sliced summer tomatoes epitomizes the kind of light lunch or late-night supper we often make for ourselves. Our midsummer gardens are full, so it's easy to run out and pick a big handful of *fines herbes*—parsley, tarragon, chervil, and chives—to use in this favorite omelet. It is a perfectly plain French classic. Why mess with a good thing?

3 eggs
Splash of milk
2 tablespoons butter, plus a little more for finishing the omelet
Small handful of your favorite grated cheese

Small handful chopped fresh *fines herbes* (parsley, tarragon, chervil, chives)
Salt and pepper

Lightly beat the eggs and milk together with a fork in a small bowl. Melt the butter in a well-seasoned or nonstick medium skillet over medium heat. When the butter is foaming, pour in the eggs. Cook, allowing them to set slightly in the skillet. Then tilting the skillet, use a spatula to gently lift the edge of the omelet, allowing the uncooked eggs to run underneath. Repeat on the opposite side. Reduce the heat to low. Once the eggs have set on the bottom, yet are still a bit loose on top, sprinkle the cheese and half the herbs down the center. Let the omelet cook just a bit longer so the bottom is very lightly colored to a soft golden brown. Using the spatula, fold the omelet into thirds (as you would a business letter), toward the center. Tip the omelet out of the skillet onto itself, seam side down onto a plate. Our omelets are often misshapen, so we use our fingers and tuck in any stray edges to make a nice oval shape. Rub a little softened butter over the omelet and scatter the remaining herbs on top. Season with salt and pepper.

PASTA WITH PARSLEY AND TOASTED WALNUT SAUCE
serves 4–6

Like a traditional basil pesto, this fragrant sauce is more flavorful when the tender parsley leaves, garlic, and walnuts are crushed together until smooth (crushing releases the essential oils) with a mortar and pestle rather than minced to a smooth purée in a blender. However, we wouldn't want you to pass up making this summery parsley sauce because you didn't have a mortar and pestle or the extra time it takes to make the sauce by hand, so we offer the blender method here as well.

2 cloves garlic, coarsely chopped

¼ cup toasted walnuts, coarsely chopped

Salt

2 cups packed fresh parsley leaves, coarsely chopped

¼ cup grated parmigiano-reggiano

¾ cup mild walnut oil or extra-virgin olive oil

1 pound spaghetti

For the sauce, using a mortar and pestle, crush the garlic, walnuts, and a large pinch of salt together. Add the parsley a handful at a time and continue crushing and grinding with the pestle to make a fine paste. Add the cheese, crushing it into the paste. Drizzle in the oil in a thin, steady stream, stirring constantly with a wooden spoon. Season the sauce with salt. This makes about 1 cup sauce.

To make the sauce in a blender (or food processor), grind the garlic, walnuts, a large pinch of salt, parsley, and ½ cup of the oil in the blender until smooth. Transfer the sauce to a bowl and stir in the cheese and the remaining oil. Season the sauce with salt.

Cook the spaghetti in a large pot of boiling salted water over medium-high heat until just cooked through, about 12 minutes. Drain the pasta, reserving ¼ cup of the cooking water. Toss the pasta in a large bowl with the sauce, loosening the sauce with some of the reserved cooking water. Serve with grated parmigiano-reggiano, if you like.

PARSLEY-POTATO SALAD
serves 4–6

We like to use russet potatoes in this salad for their tender, floury texture. Unlike other potato varieties, russets need to be boiled in their jackets (unpeeled) to protect the flesh from slowly disintegrating while cooking. The other advantage, of course, is that you end up with a more flavorful potato because it doesn't get waterlogged.

4 russet potatoes
1 bunch fresh parsley, leaves
    chopped
4 anchovy filets, finely chopped
Rind of ¼ preserved lemon,
    chopped

1 tablespoon capers
Juice of ½ lemon
⅓–½ cup really good extra-virgin
    olive oil
⅓ cup mayonnaise
Salt and pepper

Put the potatoes into a deep pot, cover with cold water, and bring to a boil over medium-high heat. Reduce the heat to medium and gently boil the potatoes until they are tender when pierced with the tip of a sharp knife, about 30 minutes.

Meanwhile, combine the parsley, anchovies, preserved lemon, capers, lemon juice, and olive oil in a medium bowl and set aside.

Drain and peel the potatoes when they are cool enough to handle, then slice them into fat rounds. Layer the potatoes in a medium bowl, buttering each slice with a little mayonnaise, then spooning some of the parsley vinaigrette between each layer and on top. Season with salt and pepper.

Luncheon Salads

SALMON SALAD
serves 4–6

Summer is wild salmon season. These fish can be pricey, but their texture and flavor make them well worth it. Throw a little extra salmon on the grill and make this salad (omitting the poaching part) with the leftovers.

1 pound salmon filet
Salt
1 small clove garlic
2 tablespoons minced chives

Rind of 1 small preserved lemon, finely chopped
¼ cup really good extra-virgin olive oil
Pepper

Put the salmon in a pan of salted water and bring to a boil over medium heat. Reduce the heat to keep the water at a gentle simmer. Poach until the salmon is just cooked, about 20 minutes. Peel off and discard the skin, then add the salmon to a bowl. Break up the flesh with a fork.

Mash the garlic to a paste, then transfer to the bowl. Add the chives, lemon rind, olive oil, and a few grinds of pepper and mix everything together.

HALIBUT SALAD
serves 4–6

We first had a version of this salad for lunch at the Gustavus Inn at Glacier Bay in Alaska more than twenty years ago. It was a simple fresh fish salad save that the halibut came from a 100-pound fish caught in the nearby Icy Straits. That memorable fish left quite an impression—we still make the salad.

1 pound halibut, poached
3 ribs celery, finely chopped
3 scallions, finely chopped
Juice of 1 lemon

⅓ cup mayonnaise
2 tablespoons sour cream
Salt and pepper
Chopped parsley

Mix the halibut, celery, scallions, lemon juice, mayonnaise, and sour cream together in a large bowl. Season with salt and pepper. Garnish with parsley.

CANAL HOUSE CURRIED CHICKEN SALAD
serves 4

We like the slightly retro flavor of this mildly curried salad. The chewy little currants add just the right note of sweetness. Our friend Maya Kaimal (who makes and sells the most delicious Indian food) grinds her own spices the traditional way, but she also recommends Sun Brand Madras Curry Powder.

¼ cup mayonnaise
½ teaspoon good curry powder
1 whole cooked boneless skinless
  chicken breast, torn into small pieces

¼ cup currants
2 tablespoons minced chives
Salt and pepper

Mix together the mayonnaise and the curry powder in a large bowl. Add the chicken, currants, and chives and fold together with a rubber spatula. Season with salt and pepper. Serve as a sandwich or as a salad on a bed of Bibb lettuce.

SHRIMP SALAD
serves 4–6

Serve this smoky rich shrimp salad—kind of an Iberian potted shrimp—on toast. Make the chunky version or the smooth, refined one.

1 pound boiled shrimp, peeled,
  deveined, and chopped
3 tablespoons minced chives
1 small clove garlic, smashed and
  minced into a paste

½ teaspoon pimentón dulce
6 tablespoons softened salted Irish
  butter, or a high-fat European-
  style butter
Pepper

Mix together the shrimp, chives, garlic, pimentón, butter, and pepper in a large mixing bowl. Or, process everything in a food processor until almost smooth. Spread on toast, grilled vegetables, or fish or add a big dollop to cooked spaghetti and toss until well mixed.

Overleaf: top row, left to right: Chopped Ham Salad with Hard-Boiled Eggs, Shrimp Salad, Canal House Curried Chicken Salad; bottom row, left to right: Salmon Salad, Halibut Salad

CHOPPED HAM SALAD WITH HARD-BOILED EGGS
makes about 4 cups

The beloved smoked ham on the bone is something we often serve at big gatherings (come to think of it, a nice big ham is like the perfect party guest: she doesn't require much fussing over, is versatile and can mingle with everyone, is never out of season, and has lots to offer). However, it's inevitable that there will be leftovers. This chopped ham salad is one way we like to use them up. We add hard-boiled eggs but never sweet relish—not that that's a bad thing, it's just our preference. Use a good ham; it really makes a difference.

1 pound cooked ham, finely diced
4 hard-boiled eggs, peeled
6 scallions, chopped

3 tablespoons Dijon mustard
1/3–1/2 cup mayonnaise
Salt and pepper

Put the ham in a medium bowl. Press 2 of the hard-boiled eggs through a sieve into the bowl. Add the scallions, mustard, and mayonnaise, and mix well. Season to taste with salt and pepper. Slice the remaining 2 hard-boiled eggs and garnish the ham salad with them.

ANYTIME EGG SALAD
makes 2½ cups or 8 open-faced sandwiches

If you always have eggs and a jar of mayonnaise, you'll always have lunch. We like to spread this salad on very thin dark rye or pumpernickel bread and then serve the open-faced sandwiches for breakfast or lunch.

Mash 10 hard-boiled eggs with the tines of a fork into small chunks in a medium bowl. Stir in ½ cup mayonnaise and 2 teaspoons Dijon mustard. Season with salt and pepper and mix well. Garnish the salad with chopped fresh parsley, chives, dill, or tarragon.

VARIATION: Mix 1½ tablespoons Madras curry powder into the egg salad.

the big reds

TOMATO TART
serves 4–6

 We usually make this simple tart with large ripe tomatoes in season, tucking some halved supersweet cherry tomatoes in between the slabs. But we've found that using even those hothouse varieties—a little more acidic and certainly less juicy—can be quite delicious, too. Eat this tart warm or at room temperature, but definitely the same day you make it as the crisp, delicate crust becomes limp if left to sit too long.

1 sheet puff pastry, defrosted
2–3 tomatoes, cored and sliced
2–3 branches fresh thyme
Really good extra-virgin olive oil

Pepper
Salt, preferably Maldon or other
 crunchy sea salt

Preheat the oven to 375°. Lay the sheet of puff pastry out on a parchment paper–lined baking sheet. Using the tip of a paring knife, lightly score a border about ½ inch from the edge of the pastry. Prick the dough inside the border all over with the tines of a fork to prevent it from puffing up too much during baking.

Arrange the tomatoes on the pastry in a single layer (crowding or overlapping the tomatoes will make the puff pastry soggy). Strip the branches of thyme, scattering the leaves over the tomatoes. Drizzle the tart with some olive oil and season with pepper.

Bake the tart until the pastry is crisp and deeply browned on the bottom and around the edges, 30–40 minutes. Season with salt.

SLICED TOMATO SALAD WITH BLUE CHEESE
(and anchovies, please!)
serves 1–2

The Homestead Inn in nearby Trenton, New Jersey, is a classic old-time Italian-American restaurant where we occasionally treat ourselves to lunch. They prepare beautifully unadorned, home-style dishes served on thick, worn white plates. As is the custom there, we start our meal off with a few of their vegetable salads, sometimes the cauliflower or the string bean, but always with the tomato salad in the summer and always with the anchovy option. Their tomato salad inspired this one.

1 small clove garlic, minced
1 tablespoon red wine vinegar
Salt and pepper
3–4 tablespoons really good
  extra-virgin olive oil

2 big fat slices of a ripe summer
  tomato
1 slice blue cheese
2 anchovy filets

Put the garlic and vinegar into a small bowl and season with salt and pepper. Stir in the olive oil and adjust the seasonings.

Arrange the sliced tomatoes on a plate and spoon the dressing over them. Place the blue cheese and anchovies on top. Season the salad with a little more salt and pepper and garnish the plate (our conceit, we can't help ourselves) with a sprig of parsley, if you like.

TOMATOES TAKE A WARM OIL BATH
makes as many as you want to make

These tomatoes, just barely warmed through in a fragrant bath of olive oil, are about as sensuous as can be. We use really big, ripe, fleshy tomatoes and treat each one like a piece of meat, carving off thick slabs and serving them with a spoonful of the oil before moving on to slicing the next. We like the flavor of fresh basil to infuse the oil. Rosemary or thyme are good, too. Though these tomatoes can be prepared on top of the stove, we often make them in a paella pan outside over an open fire to catch a little smoke.

Pour enough good extra-virgin olive oil in a deep, wide, heatproof pan to reach a depth of about 1 inch. Add several whole branches fresh basil and 3–5 crushed garlic cloves. Gently warm the oil over low heat until it is fragrant but not too hot. Add large ripe whole tomatoes stem side down in the pan. Don't crowd the tomatoes. Briefly warm them by basting them in the oil for a few minutes. Remove the pan from the heat. Slice the tomatoes into thick slabs, serving them as you carve. Spoon some of the oil over the slices and season with salt. Serve with good crusty bread to sop up more of the fragrant oil from the pan.

RED PEPPERS STUFFED WITH TOMATOES
makes 4 half peppers

One of my favorite places to eat Italian food is in London. After all, one of the best cookbooks on the subject (in my humble opinion) was written by the decidedly British Elizabeth David in 1954, *Italian Food* (Penguin Classics,1999). Back in the days when I was roaming around the world, I made it a point to fly through Heathrow whenever I headed to Europe. Timing it right, we could take a big black taxicab into the city and lunch at Bibbendum before catching an afternoon flight on to Venice, Barcelona, or some other wonderful place. Simon Hopkinson was the chef at the time and he made a version of these Piedmontese stuffed peppers from David's book. This is my memory of the dish. ——CH

2 red bell peppers
2 big ripe tomatoes
¼ cup really good olive oil
1 tablespoon vinegar (sherry, red wine, or apple balsamic)
⅓ cup currants or raisins
12 oil-cured black olives, pits removed
1 clove garlic, sliced
4 oil-packed anchovy filets
Salt and pepper

Preheat the oven to 300°. Slice the peppers in half through the stems but leave the stems attached for presentation. Remove the seeds and any white pith on the ribs. Peel the tomatoes, then cut them into quarters. Remove the seeds. Put the tomatoes in a bowl with the olive oil, vinegar, currants, and olives, and toss everything together.

Arrange the peppers in a shallow baking dish. First spoon just the currants, olives, and the dressing into the peppers, dividing them equally. Then tuck two tomato quarters into each pepper. Push a slice of garlic and an anchovy filet beneath the tomatoes. Season with salt and pepper and bake for 1 hour. Serve warm or at room temperature.

RED TOMATO PRESERVES
makes 4–6 half-pints

The tomato is, after all, a fruit. Actually, it is one of the most luscious fruits around. We will be preserving them every which way this summer while gardens and farmers' markets are full up with the lovelies.

5 pounds ripe tomatoes

2 cups granulated cane sugar

Rind and juice of 2 lemons

A fat 3-inch finger fresh ginger, peeled and thinly sliced

1 stick cinnamon

Plunge tomatoes into a pot of boiling water for 20 seconds to loosen their skins. Remove the tomatoes from the pot and when cool enough to handle, peel off the skin. Halve tomatoes crosswise and squeeze out the seeds. Put tomatoes, sugar, lemon rind and juice, ginger, and cinnamon into a large, heavy pot. Cook over medium-high heat until it comes to a boil, stirring from time to time with a wooden spoon to keep the sugar from burning while it melts. Stir gently so the fruit doesn't break up too much. Reduce heat to low and gently simmer until tomatoes look slightly translucent and the liquid has thickened, about 1 hour. Using a slotted spoon, divide the tomatoes between 4–6 hot sterilized jars. Increase the heat to high and reduce the juices until thick and syrupy, about 5 minutes more. Remove the cinnamon stick. Divide the syrup between the jars and seal. Allow the jars to cool undisturbed for several hours. These preserves will keep in the refrigerator for a few months.

To preserve the tomatoes for a longer shelf life, process them in a hot water bath. Pack the tomatoes into hot, sterilized half-pint jars. Ladle the hot syrup over the tomatoes, leaving ¼-inch headspace. Wipe the rims of the jars clean, then place sterilized lids on top and screw on the rings.

Use tongs to put the jars into a canning pot. Fill the pot with enough water to cover the lids by 2 inches. Bring to a boil and continue to boil for 15 minutes. Use tongs to carefully remove the jars from the water; place on a kitchen towel. Allow the jars to cool completely, undisturbed, before you move them. If a jar doesn't seal you can repeat the water bath process or simply refrigerate and use it.

Right out of the Garden

SIMPLE SUMMER VEGETABLES

In the summertime the farm markets, roadside stands, and our gardens are full of vegetables ready for picking and eating. We like to keep our preparations simple—why muck up all those fresh flavors? Everything gets seasoned with lots of good salt and cracked pepper. We use vegetable oil for deep frying and the best extra-virgin olive oil that we can afford to dress salads and finish dishes. Fresh and preserved lemons are a must. And salted Kerrygold Irish butter is our choice for sautéing and buttering. Here are some ways we love to serve our summer vegetables.

BEETS——we always roast our beets; it concentrates their earthy sweetness. Then we serve them...sliced with hard-boiled eggs and dressed with oil, vinegar, and chives...with grilled onions and walnut oil...with butter and tarragon...cold with an arugula salad...with feta and chives...

BROCCOLI——steamed and dressed with anchovy butter...in florets, sautéed in olive oil, with garlic and red pepper flakes...sautéed and tossed with penne...

CARROTS——cooked in butter and tossed with lots of fresh mint...stewed in olive oil then dressed with mint and vinegar...

CAULIFOWER—— boiled and served with brown butter and bread crumbs...grated and sautéed in butter...blanched, dipped in egg batter, then fried in oil flavored with garlic...stewed with chickpeas and cumin...pickled...warm with garlic mayonnaise

CELERY——chopped, tossed with vinaigrette, and served with blue cheese...poached, then bathed in an anchovy vinaigrette...celery root remoulade

SWISS CHARD——sautéed in olive oil with lemon...cooked, drizzled with cream, dotted with butter, sprinkled with grated cheese, then browned under the broiler... sautéed in olive oil and butter...sautéed and served on toast topped with a poached egg

CORN——creamed...cooked kernels, lima beans, and parsley, tossed in vinaigrette...cooked with string beans...cooked with tomatoes and cream and topped with crispy bread crumbs...sautéed with chanterelles...grilled in its husk then slathered with an herb butter

CUCUMBERS——sliced with chopped mint and rice wine vinegar...seeded, chunked, and sautéed in butter...thinly sliced and layered with paper-thin sliced red onion dressed with red wine vinegar, olive oil, and cracked black pepper...grated, salted, drained, and tossed with minced garlic mint, and Greek yogurt...chunks with tomato wedges, feta, black olives, olive oil, vinegar and oregano (the authentic Greek salad)

EGGPLANT——roasted in its skin, scooped out, and mashed with garlic and walnut oil...sliced, fried, and served with crumbled feta

FENNEL——thinly sliced with lemon, olive oil, and parmesan...roasted with bread crumbs and grated cheese...poached with lots of green olives...à la Grecque...

OKRA——dipped in buttermilk, rolled in cornmeal, and deep fried...stewed with tomatoes...pickled

SCALLIONS——grilled with Romesco Sauce (page 121)...sautéed in butter with lemon and lots of chopped parsley, served as is or piled on toast and topped with a poached egg or spooned on grilled or poached fish

STRING BEANS——boiled together with potatoes...boiled and served with tomato wedgesand vinaigrette...cooked and served warm with grated raw tomato vinaigrette...cooked with gnocchi...

POTATOES——cooked in chicken stock or milk with minced chives...

PEAS——buttered with loads of chopped mint...mashed with butter, chives, and topped with crisp bacon...raw right out of the pods...

RADISHES——buttered...sliced in open-faced sandwiches...with anchovy butter

TOMATOES——broiled with grated aged white cheddar and pepper... sliced peeled beefsteaks with crushed anchovies, garlic, and olive oil.... rubbed on toast...grated raw with minced garlic, olive oil, and red wine vinegar to spoon over grilled vegetables, fish, meat, pasta...chopped and cooked in butter with lots of chopped basil...peeled and seeded, stewed with peeled and seeded peppers in olive oil and butter, with garlic and basil (peperonata)

ZUCCHINI——sliced paper-thin and dressed with olive oil and grated pecorino...deep-fried slices...fritters...little ones poached in olive oil...halved and grilled...provençal style...

ZUCCHINI BLOSSOMS——dipped in a thin batter of flour and white wine, and deep-fried...stuffed with fresh ricotta and deep-fried...

GRILLED LEEKS WITH ROMESCO SAUCE
serves 4–6

The sweetness of a sturdy leek needs to be coaxed out by heat and one way we love to do this in the summer is to grill them whole over an open fire. The tough bluish-green outer leaves protect the pale green-white heart from the intensity of the heat. We like to serve these with romesco sauce the way the Catalans do when they grill *calçots*, their long leeklike onion, in Spain.

8–12 leeks, roots trimmed   Salt
Really good extra-virgin olive oil   1–2 cups Romesco Sauce (page 121)

Prepare a hot charcoal grill. Slice the leeks nearly in half lengthwise, starting 2–3 inches above the root end and up through the tough green top. Rinse well under cold running water to remove any sand and dirt. Rub some olive oil over the leeks and season them with salt.

Grill the leeks over red-hot coals until the outer leaves are charred. Move them to a cooler spot on the grill, piling them on top of each other, and continue grilling until the white root end feels tender. The leeks may take 30 minutes to cook, depending on their thickness and the heat of the coals.

Put the leeks on a platter, drizzle with olive oil, and sprinkle with salt. Eat the tender center with romesco sauce, discarding the charred and tough outer leaves.

POACHED LEEKS VINAIGRETTE

When we find bunches of beautiful small to medium leeks at the market, we honor the noble *Allium* by preparing this classic dish.

Remove the tough outer leaves of 6 leeks. Trim off the roots and all but 3–4 inches of the green tops. Slice the leeks nearly in half lengthwise, starting a few inches above the root end and up through the pale green top. Rinse under cold running water to remove any sand. Put the leeks into a large sauté pan. Add 2 bay leaves, 1 branch fresh thyme, 1 big pinch salt, 2 cups chicken stock, 1 cup white wine, and enough water to just cover the leeks. Bring to a simmer over medium heat. Reduce heat to medium-low, partially cover, and poach the leeks until tender when pierced with the tip of a knife, 10–15 minutes

continued on page 74

depending on how thick they are. Using a slotted spatula, transfer the leeks to a rack to drain. Wrap the leeks in a clean dishcloth and refrigerate until well chilled (they will keep in the fridge for up to 2 days).

For the vinaigrette, mash 1 small clove garlic with salt and pepper in a small bowl. Stir in 1 tablespoon Dijon mustard and 3 tablespoons red wine vinegar. Stir in ½ cup really good extra-virgin olive oil. Adjust seasonings.

Arrange leeks on a serving platter, green tops aligned. Spoon the vinaigrette over the leeks, season with salt and pepper, and garnish with 1 finely chopped hard-boiled egg and a good handful chopped fresh parsley. ——*serves 4–6*

GRILLED EGGPLANT WITH MINT
serves 4–6

We grill whole large globe eggplants over hot coals (and sometimes directly on a bed of medium-hot coals) until they collapse completely, then scrape the soft flesh out of its leathery skin to make baba ghanoush or other seasoned spreads. But we grill a smaller, narrower globe or long, thin Japanese eggplant when we want to eat them skin and all.

8 small narrow globe or Japanese eggplants, halved lengthwise	Extra-virgin olive oil
Salt	2 cloves garlic, smashed
2 lemons	1–2 pinches red pepper flakes
	1 large handful mint leaves, chopped

Put the eggplant in a large bowl, season with salt, the juice of 1 of the lemons, and a generous glug of olive oil. Turn the eggplant until well coated.

Prepare a medium-hot charcoal grill. Grill the eggplant cut side down without moving them until they are well browned with good grill marks and can be moved without sticking to the grill, about 5 minutes. Turn them over and grill the other side until the flesh is tender, about 5 minutes. Transfer the eggplant back to the bowl with the marinade and squeeze the juice from the remaining lemon over them. Add the garlic, red pepper flakes, mint, and plenty of olive oil. Toss until well coated and season with salt. Serve warm or at room temperature.

Overleaf: Lillie Anderson shopping at the Ottsville Farmers' Market in Bucks County, PA

ON A HIG

As more and more of us suffer stress
to find ways to not only relax on holi
ourselves. A new type of holiday wh
altitude training is available in the

'n-two-three: out-two-three':
my breathing follows that of
Heinz, the trainer who is
leading our group of five up the
mountain path. The pace is slow
and steady; I have to curb an
urge to pass those in front and
accelerate up to my normal
speed. Heinz, however, has
explained that climbing more
slowly is better for the body.
So, I relax into the rhythm
and enjoy the panorama of
meadows, mountain peaks and,
far below, Lech am Arlberg,
voted 'Most Beautiful Village in
Europe 2004'.

The western slopes of the
Arlberg mountain range are one
of the most majestic landscapes
in Europe. Most visitors ski her
in winter or hike in summer.
We are on a Welltain cour
This hybrid of 'Wellness
Mountain' is a new kin
holiday. Austrian spor
scientists have long k
sportsmen and wom
from altitude training,
ordinary folk gain from

totally natural wa
First comes a te
fitness — or lack
standing on a Dr
machine for a c
out comes the t
body fat, water
Thanks to swim
yoga, my repor
though I need t
muscle. Next co
minute step tes
good but could
By contrast, th
husband's lazy
exposed: he ne
pounds and bu
is given a hear
he wea

o Bregenz are Friedrichshafen, Germany (20 miles/32 km), served by Ryanair
ernatively Zurich, Switzerland (80 miles/132 km) is served by Easyjet
ss Air (www.swiss.com). See page 22 for more details.

le buses go from Friedrichshafen to Bregenz (40mins, €6). There are also
Lech (3h 10mins, €45, www.artbergexpress.com), and also direct train
to Bregenz.

rg, with buses serving every valley. Most towns operate municipal bus
aily, weekly or monthly tickets valid on all public transport systems.

one of the best restaurants in Austria. Chef-owner Heino Huber's
n, has a medieval staircase leading to 13 bedrooms. The wine cellar
. From €295 per room for two people including breakfast. Deuring
47800, www.deuring-schloessle.com
sthof Hirschen is covered in wood shingles, typical of the
ere, a genuine welcome and traditional dishes. From €80 per
Gasthof Hirschen, 6867 Schwarzenberg. 0043 5512 29440.

rtable, modern family-run hotel in the village. From €65 per
am Arlberg. 0043 5583 2382, www.hotelaustria.com
ual hotels offering Welltain treatments see their websites
h.com, bergmaehder.at, burghotel.at, derberghof.at,
hotelaustria.com, pfefferkorns.net, postlech.com,
hof.at

g.cc; info@vtour.at
: info@lech-zuers.at

proves, we
of body fat,
important
e in
anging
insists

And I still use that breathing;
only nowadays, it's when I walk
up the escalators in tube stations
or run for a bus!
KATHY ARNOLD

This year, Welltain holidays in Lech
run from 9 July to 16 September.
Courses cost €99 for a weekend,
€400 for 6 days, €700 for two
weeks. Welltain hotels, such as
the Hotel Austria, offer 6 nights
accommodation with half-board
and Welltain course from €790 per
person. Transport is not included.
For more information: Lech Zürs

transport on cable cars, chair lifts
and buses, as well as some guided
walks, the outdoor 'forest' pool, the
Lech Golf Academy, tennis, squash
and child care at Kids Active.

Gone Fishin'

the number of red blood cells in
your body. But, the Welltain
programme also helps with
everything from stress-busting
to weight loss — and all in a

...or thre...
are vital

EXERCISE AT ALTITUDE, BUT THEN ENJOY A RELAXING SPA BATH

HALIBUT AND LENTILS WITH FENNEL
serves 4

This is the quintessential surf-n-turf—the clean meaty taste of halibut balanced against the earthy flavor of lentils. Use small lentils like the little brown ones from Umbria or France's green du Puy lentils.

FOR THE LENTILS
Olive oil
1 yellow onion, minced
1 clove garlic
1 cup French or Italian lentils
1 big sprig thyme
1 tablespoon ground fennel seeds
2 cups chicken stock, fish stock, or water
Finely chopped preserved lemon rind (optional)

Salt and pepper

FOR THE HALIBUT AND FENNEL
Salt
1½ pounds halibut filet, cut into 4 thick pieces
1 fresh fennel bulb, finely chopped
Juice of 1 lemon
Really good extra-virgin olive oil
Pepper

For the lentils, heat the olive oil in a heavy pan over medium heat. Add the onions and garlic and cook, stirring occasionally, until soft, about 10 minutes. Add the lentils, thyme, ground fennel, and chicken stock. Bring to a simmer, then reduce the heat to low, cover, and cook until the lentils are tender, about 1 hour and 20 minutes. Add more stock or water if needed during cooking. Add the lemon rind to taste, if using. Season with salt and pepper.

For the halibut and fennel, fill a deep, medium pan with water and season with a big pinch of salt. Put the halibut into the water and bring to a gentle simmer over medium heat. Adjust the heat to keep the water barely bubbling. Poach the fish for 20 minutes. Remove the fish from the water with a fish spatula.

While the halibut poaches, put the fennel into a bowl and dress with lemon juice and a good drizzle of olive oil. Season with salt and pepper. Taste and adjust seasonings, if necessary.

Spoon the lentils onto a large platter or individual plates. Place the halibut on the lentils then scatter fennel over the fish. Drizzle everything with olive oil.

SALMON WITH LEMON-BUTTER SAUCE
serves 4

This year, we've been eating our salmon and asparagus bathed in a luxurious lemony butter sauce, similar to hollandaise but better—fresher tasting, not so cloyingly thick. We first learned how delicious it was at Ballymaloe with Darina Allen—the high priestess of Irish cuisine. It relies on the salted Irish butter we're so crazy about from Kerrygold—but other brands of European-style high-fat butter will suit.

FOR THE LEMON-BUTTER SAUCE
2 large egg yolks
8 tablespoons (1 stick) cold
   Irish butter, cut into 8 pieces
1 tablespoon lemon juice
Salt

FOR THE SALMON
Salt
1½ pounds wild salmon,
   cut into 4 pieces
Fresh tarragon leaves, chopped
Fresh chives, minced

Whisk together the egg yolks and 1 tablespoon water in a medium, heavy-bottomed saucepan. Cook over low heat, whisking continuously so the yolks don't "scramble". Add the butter a tablespoon at a time, whisking to melt each into the sauce before adding the next. If the sauce begins to separate, remove the pan from the heat and whisk in another piece of the cold butter to cool the sauce down. It should come back together. Return the pan to the heat and continue whisking in the butter one piece at time until it has all been incorporated. Remove from heat and whisk in the lemon juice. Season with salt. Keep the sauce warm by setting the pan in a larger pan of hot water.

Fill another pan with salted water, add the salmon, and simmer over medium heat until the fish is just cooked, about 20 minutes. Using a fish spatula, transfer the salmon to a platter or individual plates. Spoon the lemon-butter sauce over the fish and serve garnished with tarragon and chives.

KIPPERS
for one person, increase accordingly

How funny, a friend who once edited the fashion pages of the *Times, Elle &
Co.* in times gone by when periodicals had great worth and celebrity was an
amusing novelty and quality was to the fore, asked me to write about kip-
pers for a magazine he edited and published in a one-man-show…anyhow,
all quite lovely stuff. Alan Davidson wrote a book titled *A Kipper With My
Tea*. No sensationalism there, just delights.

The kipper makes for great eating. There are two methods that deliver beautifully. Here are both for you to try, choose your favourite. —— *Jeremy Lee*

1 kipper   Slices of good brown bread
A nob of unsalted butter   A pat of unsalted butter
2 rashers of very best streaky bacon
1 freshest egg

Preheat the oven to 400°. Place the kipper, the skin side down, upon a cast-
iron pan. Spread this with the nob of butter. Pop this in the oven and cook
for 5 or 6 minutes until dark and golden, releasing a heavenly rich heady
aroma. Remove the pan from the oven and then lift the kipper to a warm
dish or plate. Place the pan on a gentle heat and lay in the rashers of bacon
and fry gently until cooked, just as you like it, in the kippered butter.

Fill a small pan with water and place on a high heat to boil. Crack the egg
into a teacup and lower the heat beneath the water until it simmers, stir the
water well and then tip in the egg, stirring gently to keep it whole. Let cook
for 3 minutes or so until the white sets just so, and the yolk remains soft.

Spread the slices of bread with plenty of butter and heap on a plate. Remove
the bacon to a wee plate and sit the poached egg alongside. Place all on the table and eat all as best suits your mood, say a forkful or two of kipper heaped on
buttered bread with a piece of bacon rasher, the dainty dipped in the poached
egg. Freshly brewed tea is vital to complete this estimable repast.

VARIATION: Place 1 kipper in a large dish, earthenware or good old Pyrex
perform admirably here. Boil a kettle of water. Pour the boiling water over

the kipper, just enough to cover. Weight the kipper and let stand thus for 5 or 6 minutes, another minute or two if unconvincing. Spread plenty of good brown bread with best unsalted butter. Lift the kipper from its bath and lay upon a plate, carefully remove the flesh and heap onto the buttered bread. The delicacy of the kipper cooked thus is otherworldly.

Freshly milled pepper and a drop or two of lemon juice is worth considering. Once again, tea is required. Oh yes, a glass of Guinness is rather good too.

Chef Jeremy Lee of London's Blue Print Café is our man in London.

TERRINE OF SALMON AND PEAS
serves 4–6

We've heard that some folks consider aspic retro, but for us it has never gone out of style. And anyway, summer is the season to serve this cooling recipe. Forgoing a calf's foot to gel the liquid, we use good old Knox Gelatine, but we cut down the ratio of gelatin to liquid to 1 envelope for every 2–3 cups liquid—depending on your nerve. We like our aspic delicate and trembly and don't care at all if it collapses slightly. The success of this dish relies on the quality of your fish stock.

Salt

1½ pounds wild salmon filet,
   cut into 4–6 pieces

3 cups peas

1 bunch scallions, trimmed
   and chopped

Pepper

1–2 envelopes unflavored gelatin

3 cups good, well-seasoned
   fish stock

Fill a pan with salted water, add the salmon, and bring to a simmer over medium heat until the fish is just cooked, about 20 minutes. Using a fish spatula, transfer the salmon to a plate. When the salmon is cool enough to handle, remove and discard the skin.

Cook the peas and the scallions in a pot of salted water over medium-high heat until just tender, about 3 minutes. Drain, season with salt and pepper, and transfer to a bowl to cool.

Soften gelatin in 2–3 tablespoons cool water in a medium bowl. Add ½ cup hot fish stock and stir until the gelatin has dissolved. Stir in 2½ cups of cool fish stock.

Put 1 cup peas and scallions into a 6-cup terrine, arrange the salmon pieces on top, then add the remaining peas and scallions, making sure that they fill in the spaces around and on top of the salmon. Pour the stock into the terrine. Cover and refrigerate until set, at least 4 hours.

Unmold gently onto a long platter. The aspic may be soft and collapse slightly but that will be a testament to its delicacy.

The Bird is the Word

ROASTED CHICKEN WITH TOMATO BUTTER
serves 4–6

We add lovely fishy-flavored oil-packed anchovies to our Tomato Butter to infuse it with salty subtle flavor. We slather it on everything. The delicate Tomato Butter Sauce is delicious spooned over poached fish or eggs.

FOR THE TOMATO BUTTER

2 anchovy filets

6 sprigs fresh thyme

¾ cup sherry

2 big tablespoons tomato paste

8 tablespoons (1 stick) cold butter, cut into 6 pieces

FOR THE CHICKEN

1 whole chicken, 3–5 pounds, back removed (see page 97)

Salt and pepper

Chopped fresh parsley

Chopped fresh rosemary

For the tomato butter, put the anchovies, thyme, and sherry into a saucepan and bring to a simmer over medium-high heat. Gently simmer for 15 minutes. Strain, discard the solids, and return the sherry to the pan. Bring to a boil and cook until the sherry has reduced to ¼ cup.

Whisk in the tomato paste, then add the butter one piece at a time, whisking continuously, until all the butter has been used and the sauce is smooth. Keep warm over a pot of simmering water, or cool and refrigerate.

For the chicken, preheat the oven to 400°. Wipe the chicken dry with paper towels. Put the chicken on a rack in a roasting pan. Rub with salt and pepper. Roast until the juices run clear when you pierce the thigh with a sharp knife, 45–60 minutes. Remove from oven, and allow chicken to rest for about 15 minutes. Cut the chicken into pieces, arrange on a platter, and spoon or slather with lots of tomato butter. Garnish with parsley and rosemary.

VARIATION: To make Tomato Butter Sauce, follow the Tomato Butter recipe through the first step above. Whisk 2 egg yolks and 1 tablespoon water together in a bowl. Whisk the yolks and 2 big tablespoons tomato paste into the reduced sherry. Cook over low heat, whisking continuously so the yolks don't "scramble". Add 8 tablespoons cold butter, cut into 6 pieces, 1 piece at a time, whisking until it has melted before adding the next. If the sauce separates, remove from heat and whisk in another piece of cold butter. It should come back together. Return to heat and continue whisking in butter one piece at a time.

ROASTED CHICKEN SMOTHERED IN CHANTERELLES
serves 4–6

We were having one of those hot, muggy summers, typical for our river valley, but we'd had so much rain that this one was going on the record as one of the wettest. Most of the local produce tasted watery, plus the tomatoes were suffering from a terrible blight. The silver lining was the bumper crop of chanterelles we found in the woods that season. We gathered so many with such little effort that we were eating them morning, noon, and night.

One evening we had an impromptu supper at Canal House, friends just kept dropping by. Soon there were ten of us to feed with only one roasted chicken. It looked so paltry on the platter. Then we remembered—how could we be so blasé?—the grocery bag full of chanterelles we had gathered that day. We sautéed all the mushrooms and piled them on top of the bird. Our little supper turned into a feast, with all those meaty mushrooms, we hardly even needed that chicken after all.

1 chicken, 3–5 pounds
2 tablespoons extra-virgin olive oil
1 lemon
Salt and pepper
6 tablespoons butter

1–2 cloves garlic, thinly sliced
2 pounds chanterelles, cleaned
   and halved or quartered
Leaves of 1 bunch fresh parsley,
   chopped

Preheat the oven to 400°. Rinse the chicken and pat it dry with paper towels. Rub it with olive oil and the juice of the lemon, then season it well with salt and pepper. Put the chicken on a rack in a roasting pan. Roast until the juices run clear when you pierce the thigh with a sharp knife, 45–60 minutes. Remove the chicken from the oven and let it rest for about 15 minutes.

Meanwhile, melt the butter in a large skillet over medium-high heat. Add the garlic and the mushrooms. Season with salt and pepper. Sauté the mushrooms, stirring often, until they are tender and have released their juices, 5–10 minutes. Take the mushrooms off the heat and stir in the parsley. Adjust the seasonings.

Cut the chicken into pieces and arrange on a serving platter. Pile the mushrooms on top of the chicken. Pour any remaining chicken juices over the mushrooms. Serve with thick slices of toasted crusty bread to sop up the juices, if you like.

TURKEY GALANTINE
(without the aspic)
serves 10–12

We like to use a skin-on boneless turkey breast (often sold as "turkey breast roast") rather than a skinless one when making this recipe because the skin adds a little more flavor to the sweet mildness of turkey. Once the breast is poached, the skin is removed. We serve this elegant galantine cold with our herbal Summer Mayonnaise rather than with a traditional aspic accompaniment.

6 ounces ground veal

6 ounces ground pork

Leaves of 1 bunch fresh parsley, chopped

2 scallions, white parts only, minced

Leaves of 2 sprigs fresh tarragon, chopped

Small bunch fresh chives, chopped

1 egg

Salt and pepper

1 boneless turkey breast half (about 3 pounds)

2 celery ribs, halved

2 carrots, peeled

1 onion, halved

1 bay leaf

2 cups Summer Mayonnaise (page 43)

Put the veal, pork, parsley, scallions, tarragon, chives, egg, and a generous seasoning of salt and pepper in a medium bowl and mix well. Set the stuffing aside.

Lay the turkey breast skin side down on a cutting board. Using a large sharp knife, slice through the breast lengthwise, parallel to the board, almost all the way through so that breast opens up like a book. Spread the stuffing evenly over the meat. Close the breast up again to enclose the stuffing. Place the breast on a large piece of cheesecloth. Wrap it around well, making sure the breast encloses all the stuffing, then tie the breast into a neat package with kitchen string.

Put the breast into a large pot. Add the celery, carrots, onions, bay leaf, and a generous pinch of salt and cover with cold water by at least 2 inches. Bring to a boil over medium-high heat, then reduce the heat to maintain a gentle

continued

simmer. Poach the breast until it reaches an internal temperature of 155°, about 1 hour. Remove the pot from the heat and let the galantine cool in the poaching liquid. Remove it from the liquid, cover tightly with plastic wrap, and refrigerate until well chilled (the galantine will keep like this for up to 4 days). Strain the turkey broth and save it for another use, if you like.

Unwrap the galantine, then peel off and discard the skin. Carve it into ½-inch-thick slices. Serve with the mayonnaise.

PANKO FRIED CHICKEN WITH LEMON
serves 6–8

We are chicken thigh lovers, especially when it comes to fried chicken—the flavorful dark meat stays moist while the crumbed outside has a chance to get crisp and golden. These little boneless half-thigh pieces coated in extra crunchy Japanese bread crumbs fry up evenly and quickly.

Vegetable oil

8–10 boneless chicken thighs (with or without skin), cut in half

3 eggs, beaten

4 cups panko

Salt

2 lemons, cut into wedges

Add enough oil to a large cast-iron skillet to reach a depth of 1–2 inches. Heat the oil over medium heat until it is hot but not smoking, ideally to a temperature of 350° (use a candy thermometer to check the temperature).

Dip one piece of chicken at a time into the eggs, then dredge in the panko. Working in batches to avoid crowding the skillet, fry the chicken in the hot oil until golden brown all over, about 5 minutes on the first side and 3 minutes or so on the second side. Transfer the fried chicken with a slotted spoon to a wire rack set over paper towels to drain. Season with salt while still hot.

Serve hot or at room temperature with wedges of lemon for squeezing over the fried chicken just before eating.

GRILLED QUAIL & FRESH FIGS
serves 4

There's no getting around it, you've got to eat these little succulent smoky birds with your fingers. We set the platter of them in the center of the table and let everyone help themselves.

12–16 fresh figs, halved lengthwise
¼ cup balsamic vinegar
6 tablespoons really good
   extra-virgin olive oil

Salt and pepper
8 whole jumbo quail

Put the figs in a bowl. Toss them with the vinegar, 2–3 tablespoons of the oil, and some salt and pepper. Set them aside to marinate while you prepare a hot charcoal or gas grill.

Rinse the quail and pat them dry with paper towels. Rub them with a couple tablespoons of the olive oil, then season with salt and pepper. Grill the quail over a hot fire, turning them when they are well browned and a little charred in places. Take the quail off the grill when they are well browned all over and the meat is just cooked through, 5–15 minutes depending on the heat of your grill and how well done you like them.

Grill the figs while the quail are cooking. Put them on the grill cut side up over medium-hot heat, reserving marinade. Grill the figs without turning them until the flesh begins to bubble and get a little jammy but before the fruit collapses, 3–5 minutes. Return the figs to the bowl with the marinade as they are done.

Put the quail on a platter, season well with salt, and spoon the figs and juices around the birds. Drizzle with the remaining olive oil.

GRILLED SPATCHCOCKED CHICKEN
serves 4

This is a recipe for a simple grilled chicken but it includes two helpful techniques. The first is cutting the back out of the bird and splitting it open so it is more manageable as it cooks on the grill. The second is grilling a bird over indirect heat over a pan of water. This prevents flare-ups from fat dripping onto the hot coals, and ensures an evenly browned bird.

1 chicken, 3–5 pounds	Salt and pepper
2 tablespoons olive oil	1 lemon, cut in half

Rinse the chicken inside and out and pat it dry with paper towels. Using poultry shears or a sharp knife, cut along both sides for the entire length of the backbone, cutting it out completely. Save it for making stock, if you like. Lay the chicken on a clean surface skin side up and press down on it with your hands to flatten it out a bit. Rub the chicken all over with the olive oil and season it generously with salt and pepper.

Prepare a grill with a lid with charcoal for grilling over indirect heat: Pile unlit hardwood charcoal off to one side of the grill and set an aluminum pan of water off to the other side. Light the charcoal and set the grill rack in place. When the coals are white-hot, put the chicken on the grill skin side up over the pan of water. Cover it and grill the chicken until the skin is golden brown, 45–60 minutes. Keep the grill hot as the chicken cooks by adding more charcoal as needed. The chicken is finished cooking when the thigh juices run clear when pricked.

Transfer the chicken to a platter, squeeze the lemon juice over it, and season with salt and pepper. Let the chicken rest for 15 minutes before serving.

GRILLED BRANZINO

Wrapping fish in leaves before grilling protects their delicate flesh from burning and makes them easier to handle.

Have your fishmonger debone two 1½-pound branzini (heads-on) as they would a trout. Open the fish, flesh side up, and slather with Green Sauce (page 42) or

continued on page 100

scatter with chopped fresh parsley and tarragon leaves, and season with salt and pepper. Close up the fish. Cut fennel fronds and grape vines with leaves into pieces about the same length as the fish. Lay the fish on top of the fronds and vines, lay more fronds and vines on top of the fish, then use thin flexible steel wire to tie each fish into a neat package.

Grill over a medium fire, turning often, for 20 minutes. The leaves will char and blacken. Remove from the grill, cut the wire, remove the grape vines and fronds, and serve the branzini drizzled with olive oil and seasoned with salt and pepper. ——*serves 2*

GRILLED DUCK BREAST WITH PRUNES IN RED WINE
serves 4

Muscovy ducks have less fat than Pekin, so the skin get browned and crisp while the meat is still medium rare—the perfect combo.

2 Muscovy whole duck breasts, split into 4 half breasts	16 pitted prunes
Salt and pepper	2 cups red wine
	2 bay leaves

Score the duck breast, cutting through the skin and into the fat but not into the meat, in a crosshatch pattern. Season well with salt and pepper. Wrap and allow to seasonin the refrigerator for about a day.

Put the prunes, red wine, and bay leaves in a heavy medium pot. Bring to a simmer over medium heat, then reduce heat to low, cover, and gently simmer until the prunes are very soft and the wine is syrupy, about 1 hour.

Prepare a grill with charcoal for grilling over indirect heat: Pile unlit hardwood charcoal off to one side of the grill and set an aluminum pan of water off to the other side. Light the charcoal and set the grill rack in place. When the coals are white-hot, put the duck breasts on the grill skin side down over the pan of water. Grill the duck, turning several times until the skin is golden brown and has released most of its fat, about 30 minutes. Remove duck from grill and set aside on a cutting board to rest for 15 minutes.

Slice the duck breast crosswise and serve with the prunes and red wine sauce.

Overleaf: Branzini wrapped in grape vines and fennel fronds, ready for the grill

THE WHOLE BEEF TENDERLOIN, PEPPERED AND GRILLED
serves 12

For those of us who enjoy a good piece of chewy, on-the-bone, grilled steak, a filet seems kind of wimpy—the meat is so lean and mild. But it's these very qualities that make the filet the perfect choice for grilling whole and serving either warm or cold.

FOR THE BEEF
1 whole beef tenderloin
¼ cup coarsely ground black pepper
Salt

FOR THE SALAD
Juice of 1 lemon
6–8 anchovy filets, finely chopped
4–6 tablespoons really good
  extra-virgin olive oil

Salt and pepper
1 bunch arugula, torn
1 small head Bibb lettuce, torn
1 small bunch parsley, leaves
  coarsely chopped
Big handful celery leaves, chopped
Handful fresh tarragon leaves,
  chopped

For the beef, using a sharp knife, trim off any fat from the tenderloin. Slide the blade under the long sinewy silver skin, trimming it off. Fold about 6 inches of the thin end of the meat under itself. This folded over end should be about as thick as the rest of the filet so that it cooks evenly. Tie into a "neat package" with thin flexible steel wire. Rub with the pepper, pressing it into the meat, and season with salt.

Prepare a medium-hot hardwood charcoal or gas grill. Grill the filet over the hottest part of the grill, turning it as a good brown crust develops. When the meat is browned all over, move it to a cooler spot on the grill to finish cooking, turning occasionally, until the internal temperature reaches 120° for rare and 130° for medium-rare. The grilling time will vary depending on your grill and the heat. Start checking the internal temperature after 20 minutes. Take the meat off the grill and let it rest for 15 minutes. Serve warm or let it cool, then wrap and refrigerate it for up to 3 days before serving it cold and sliced.

For the salad, make the vinaigrette in the bottom of a salad bowl, stirring together the lemon juice, anchovies, olive oil, and salt and pepper to taste. Pile greens and herbs into the bowl and toss. Serve with the grilled filet.

SMOKY MUSSELS WITH TOASTED BREAD CRUMBS
makes about 60 mussels

Like the rest of America, during the summer we spend lots of time outside grilling, either over the fire pit or on our kettle grill. We take advantage of the fragrant heat and cook in pans over the fire, using heavy-gauge carbon steel paella pans (and not just for paella!) that range in size from Big Bertha, our 35-incher to a utilitarian 12-inch pan. They are perfect for cooking these mussels, which open quickly in the wide, shallow pan. The best part of cooking them over coals is the smoky flavor that they pick up. Ultimately, it's all about the sweet perfume of smoke.

Olive oil
1 onion, finely chopped
2 cloves garlic, finely chopped
1 cup white wine

3 pounds mussels, debearded
2 cups Toasted Bread Crumbs
(page 42)

Prepare a medium-hot charcoal grill. Put a large pan (we like a 16-inch paella pan) on the grill over the coals and add about 3 tablespoons olive oil, swirling it around to coat the pan. Add the onions and garlic and cook, stirring frequently, until soft, 3–5 minutes. Add the wine to the pan and cook for a minute or two. Add the mussels. Cover the pan with a lid from a grill and cook the mussels until their shells open about halfway and the flesh is plump and just cooked through, about 5 minutes. Remove the pan from the grill.

Twist off and discard the top shell from each mussel (discard any unopened mussels), making sure that the bottom shell has a mussel in it. Arrange the mussels in their shells face up in a single layer in the pan.

Drizzle a little olive oil over the mussels, then scatter the bread crumbs on top. Return the pan to the hot grill. Cover the pan with the lid for a few minutes until the mussels have heated through. Remove the pan from the heat and serve the mussels warm or at room temperature directly from the pan.

summer sweets

BERRY COBBLER
serves 4–6

Our friend Pam Anderson, the cookbook author and food columnist, can really nail a recipe. After all, she's built a career on developing perfect, delicious recipes. This cookie dough–topped cobbler recipe comes from her award-winning first cookbook *The Perfect Recipe* (Houghton Mifflin, 1998). As she writes in the introduction to the recipe, "[This] makes one of the best cobblers you'll probably ever eat." We couldn't agree with her more.

½ cup all-purpose flour
¼ teaspoon baking powder
Pinch of salt
8 tablespoons (1 stick) unsalted butter, softened
1 cup sugar

1 egg yolk
1¼ teaspoons vanilla extract
1 tablespoon cornstarch
2 pints fresh raspberries or a combination of your favorite berries

Mix together the flour, baking powder, and salt in a small bowl and set aside.

Using a wooden spoon, beat the butter and ½ cup of the sugar together in a medium mixing bowl until well combined. Beat in the egg yolk and ¼ teaspoon of the vanilla. Add the flour mixture and stir until well combined. Refrigerate the dough while preheating the oven to 375°.

Combine the remaining ½ cup sugar and the cornstarch in a medium bowl. Add the berries and the remaining 1 teaspoon vanilla and toss gently to coat.

Put the berries into an 8-inch square (or 8-cup) baking dish. Drop the dough by heaping tablespoons over the berries, covering the fruit evenly. Bake until the berries are bubbling and the topping is golden brown, about 45 minutes. Let cool slightly before serving.

VARIATION: For Italian Prune Plum Cobbler, prepare the dough as above. Substitute 1¾ pounds quartered pitted Italian prune plums for the berries and reduce the amount of cornstarch to 2 teaspoons. Replace 1 teaspoon of the vanilla extract with ½ teaspoon ground cinnamon.

TUILES
makes 2–3 dozen

These delicate curved cookies are named for the terra-cotta roof tiles seen throughout the south of France. It takes a little practice lifting them off the parchment paper once they are baked, but don't be discouraged. They are such elegant cookies and fun to make. However, we avoid making them on a humid day. They will not stay crisp.

2 egg whites, at room temperature
Pinch of salt
6 tablespoons sugar
¼ teaspoon vanilla extract
¼ teaspoon almond extract

½ cup sifted cake flour
5 tablespoons very soft (but not melted) unsalted butter
½ cup sliced blanched almonds

Preheat the oven to 350°. Line several cookie sheets with parchment paper and set aside. Set out a rolling pin to drape the warm cookies over when they come out of the oven.

Whisk together the egg whites, salt, sugar, and the vanilla and almond extracts in a medium mixing bowl until very frothy. Whisk in the flour in thirds. Whisk in the butter, a few tablespoons at a time, until the batter is smooth and opaque.

Spoon 1 tablespoon of the batter at a time onto the prepared cookie sheets, at least 3 inches apart, and use the back of the spoon in a circular motion to spread the batter out to a 3–4 inch round. The batter will look very thin and not necessarily even, but don't worry; the cookies will come out fine. Scatter some almonds over the rounds.

Bake the cookies one sheet at a time until very pale golden brown in the center and deeper brown around the edges, 8–10 minutes. Remove from the oven. Working quickly while cookies are still hot, use a thin metal spatula to lift each off the parchment paper, then drape it over the rolling pin, gently bending it with your hand to shape it into a curve. Rewarm the cookies in the oven briefly if they have cooled too much and are no longer pliable. Transfer the shaped cookies to cooling racks to finish cooling completely.

STRONG COFFEE GRANITA
makes about 1 quart

During the hot summer months, we like to end our meals with this simple sweet—dessert and espresso in a single course. A dollop of whipped cream spooned over the "grainy" coffee ice crystals adds an unexpected lusciousness to its refreshing taste. The granita will stay fresh-tasting in a covered plastic container in the freezer for up to 1 week.

1 cup sugar   Sweetened whipped cream
2 cups very strong hot coffee

Stir the sugar into the coffee until it has dissolved, then set it aside to cool. Pour the cooled coffee into a flat baking pan (about 9 × 13 inches) or a wide container that will fit on a shelf in the freezer. Slide the pan into the freezer. The liquid will become slushy around the edges within an hour or so. Scrape the granita with the tines of a fork where it is beginning to freeze. Continue stirring, scraping, and breaking up any lumps every 30 minutes, until the granita has all frozen icy crystals throughout. Serve in chilled glasses with a big spoonful of whipped cream on top.

PINK LEMON GRANITA
makes 3–4 cups

One day while making a batch of lemon granita, we noticed we had a lone blood orange on hand, so we decided to add its rosy juice to the mix—pink lemon juice! Since blood oranges are only available in the winter, we substitute pink grapefruit juice when blood oranges aren't around. The granita will stay fresh-tasting in a covered plastic container in the freezer for up to 1 week.

continued

Finely grated zest of 2 lemons
1½ cups fresh lemon juice (8–10 lemons)

Juice of 1 blood orange or ½ Ruby Red grapefruit
½ cup sugar
Sweetened whipped cream

Put the lemon zest, citrus juices, and sugar into a medium bowl and stir until the sugar dissolves completely. Pour the sweetened juice into a flat baking pan (about 9 × 13 inches) or a wide container that will fit on a shelf in the freezer. Slide the pan into the freezer. The liquid will become slushy-frozen in 1–2 hours. Scrape the granita with the tines of a fork, making frozen icy crystals throughout. Return the granita to the freezer to finish freezing, about 1 hour. Give the granita a final scrape, breaking up any icy chunks with a fork. Serve small portions in chilled glasses with a big spoonful of whipped cream on top.

ZABAIONE
serves 2–4

Even as late as the 1960s, San Francisco's North Beach was a great Italian-American neighborhood. I used to live up the hill on Union Street. Young and counting my pennies, I could eat lunch at the Caffe Malvina for twenty-five cents—ten for a slice of pizza, ten for an espresso, and five cents for a chocolate chip cookie. The splurge was to go to Vanessi's down on Broadway. We would sit at the counter and watch the show. The cooks, dressed in their crisp whites, were lined up in front of the big grill. They tossed scampi in sauté pans, flames flared as they splashed in the wine—it was great drama. We would order a platter of delicate fried zucchini served crisp in a big tangled pile and watch as the cooks turned out plate after plate of delicious food. But the showstopper was the ethereal zabaione. Grabbing a big copper bowl, a cook would deftly crack the eggs, separating yolks from whites, tossing away the shells. Wielding a big balloon whisk, he would beat air into the sticky yolks sweetened with sugar and fortified with marsala. He would pour the foamy zabaione into stemmed glasses, the froth spilling over the sides.——CH

FOR THE ZABAIONE
4 egg yolks
¼ cup sugar
¼ cup vin santo, moscato d'Asti
  or Riesling

FOR THE PEACHES
4 ripe peeled peaches, sliced
1 tablespoon sugar

Choose a pot big enough to accommodate the mixing bowl you will use to beat the yolks (see next step). Fill with enough water to come about 2 inches up the side of the pot. Bring to a low simmer over low heat.

Put the yolks into a large metal (copper if you have it) mixing bowl. Using a large balloon whisk (the larger the whisk the frothier the zabaione), beat the yolks as you gradually sprinkle in the sugar, until they are pale yellow and fluffy, about 5 minutes. Place the bowl the over barely simmering water and continue beating while you dribble in the wine. Don't allow the egg to cook on the sides of the bowl. Whisk until the zabaione falls into soft mounds, about 10 minutes.

Sugar the peaches, then divide between four bowls, and spoon zabaione on top.

Preserving Summer

PATTY CURTAN'S FAMOUS APRICOT JAM
makes about 20 pints

Royal Blenheim apricots make the best jam. The fruit tends to be small and meaty—intensely flavorful. This amount makes approximately 20 pints of jam, a one-year supply for our household use and lots to give away. I like to make the jam in two batches; after all, who has a pot that big? After a day or two, when you have admired your beautiful work enough, store it away in a cool, dark place. The jam will keep for a year or two, although it will darken in color, to no ill effect, the longer you keep it. —*Patty Curtan*

22–24 pounds very ripe, meaty apricots (1 lug box), washed
30 cups granulated cane sugar (15 pounds)
1½ cups lemon juice (about 8 lemons), strained of any seeds

Cut the apricots in half, remove the pits, and cut each half into 3 or 4 slices. Using a hammer, crack open about 24 pits, and reserve the kernels inside. Apricot kernels resemble almonds in appearance and flavor, and will deepen and enhance the apricot taste.

To make the first of two batches, measure 5 heaping quarts (20 cups) fruit and put it in a heavy, stainless 5-gallon pot. Add 15 cups of the sugar, mixing as you go. Bring the fruit to a boil over medium heat, stirring frequently with a long wooden spoon. Adjust the heat to keep the fruit simmering gently. Skim off the foam as it forms, reserving it in a bowl, allowing it to cool and settle. The thin syrup that settles to the bottom makes excellent pancake syrup or sauce, and keeps in the refrigerator for months.

Increase the heat and boil gently (just low enough to prevent being splattered), for about 20 minutes, stirring frequently, then constantly toward the end. Continue to skim off any foam. Cook until the jam reaches 220° on a candy thermometer. Add ¾ cup of the lemon juice and continue cooking and stirring for 1 minute more.

continued

Have 10 to 12 hot, sterilized pint jars, lids, and bands ready. Ladle the hot jam into a large measuring cup, or something with a handle and a spout. Put 1 apricot kernel in each jar. Fill the jars to the fill line, leaving ½-inch headspace, and wipe the edges clean. Top with the lids and screw the bands on until just tight. As the jars cool, you will hear a distinct click as a vacuum forms and pulls the lid down. Sometimes a jar will have an imperfect seal; in that case, refrigerate and use it first.

Repeat from step two and make the second batch.

Patricia Curtan is an artist and designer who lives in Northern California. She is our friend and colleague, and the loveliest cook we know.

RED CURRANT JELLY
makes about 6 half-pints

Tempted as we are to spoon this luscious old-fashioned jelly onto our morning toast, currants are hard to come by, so we treasure each beautiful jar and serve it as a condiment with grilled and roasted meats. Currants have a high level of pectin so the jelly will set beautifully.

3 quarts ripe red currants   3–6 cups granulated cane sugar

Put the currants stems and all in a large, heavy enameled cast-iron pot. Gently crush the fruit with the back of a wooden spoon. Bring to a low simmer over medium-low heat. Cook until the berries collapse slightly, lose their vibrant color, and begin to release their juice, about 1 hour.

Transfer fruit and juice to a large jelly bag suspended over a bowl. (You may have to do this in batches). Don't squeeze the bag, it could make the jelly cloudy. When the juice stops running, discard the berries. Each quart of berries should yield about 1 cup juice.

Pour the juice back into the pot, add 1 cup sugar for every 1 cup juice and bring to a boil over medium heat. Boil for about 10 minutes, skimming off any foam, until the liquid reaches 220° on a candy thermometer.

Pour the jelly into hot, sterilized half-pint jars, leaving ½-inch headspace. Wipe the edges clean, then top with the sterilized lids and screw the bands on.

continued

Use tongs to put the jars into a canning pot. Fill the pot with enough water to cover the lids by 2 inches. Bring to a boil and continue to boil for 10 minutes. Use tongs to carefully remove the jars from the water and place jars on a kitchen towel. Allow the jars to cool completely, undisturbed, before you move them. As the jars cool, you will hear a distinct click as a vacuum forms and pulls the lid down. Sometimes a jar will have an imperfect seal; in that case, refrigerate and use it first.

ROMESCO SAUCE
makes about 2 cups

Tony Knickerbocker has been feeding the who's who of Napa since 1975 when he started Knickerbockers' Catering. He shared his delicious romesco sauce with us. It keeps well in the refrigerator for up to a month so we make enough to have on hand. If the sauce separates, simply whisk the olive oil back in. If the sauce is too thick, add a little more olive oil. When there are no peppers in his garden, Tony uses jarred roasted Spanish peppers. We serve this sauce with grilled vegetables, fish, meat—in fact, with just about anything!

1 cup toasted almonds and hazelnuts
3 large roasted red bell peppers, peeled and seeded
2 teaspoons ancho chile powder
2 tablespoons tomato paste
2 cloves garlic
1 tablespoon pimentón dulce
3 tablespoons sherry or wine vinegar
Salt
¾ cup really good extra-virgin olive oil

Put the nuts in a food processor and process until finely ground. Add peppers, chile powder, tomato paste, garlic, pimentón, vinegar, and salt, and pulse a few times to make a chunky mixture. Drizzle in the olive oil while processing. Let it sit for about 15 minutes to develop the flavor. Add more salt and vinegar, if you like. Store in the refrigerator for up to 1 week.

COMPOUND BUTTERS
makes 1 cup of each

When we're grilling a beautiful piece of fish, a hunk of meat, a spatchcocked chicken (page 97), or a pile of vegetables, we usually keep the seasonings quite simple up front—some good olive oil and salt and pepper—then finish what we've grilled with any one of these flavorful compound butters, slathered on at the end. We use rich and delicious salted Irish butter because everything tastes better with it. And when we don't use the compound butter right away, we cover it up and keep it in the fridge, using it within 3–4 days, or we freeze it and use it within a month.

FRESH HERB BUTTER

Beat ½ pound (2 sticks) softened salted butter in a medium bowl with a wooden spoon until smooth and creamy. Add ½ cup chopped fresh herbs (use one or a combination of your favorite herbs), 1 small finely chopped shallot or scallion, and 1 small minced garlic clove, if you like. Season with salt and pepper, and stir until well combined.

LEMON BUTTER

Beat ½ pound (2 sticks) softened salted butter in a medium bowl with a wooden spoon until smooth and creamy. Wash and dry 2 lemons, then finely grate the zest over the butter. Squeeze in juice of ½ lemon and season with salt and pepper. Stir well to incorporate the lemon juice into the butter.

FRESH HORSERADISH BUTTER

Beat ½ pound (2 sticks) softened salted butter in a medium bowl with a wooden spoon until smooth and creamy. Add 2–3 tablespoons finely grated peeled fresh horseradish root (or 2 tablespoons drained prepared horseradish) and season generously with cracked black pepper and some salt. Stir until well combined.

PIMENTÓN BUTTER

Beat ½ pound (2 sticks) softened salted butter in a medium bowl with a wooden spoon until smooth and creamy. Add 1 tablespoon pimentón, and season with salt and pepper. Stir until well combined.

BAGNA CAUDA

Summer crudités are made all the more delicious when dipped into this warm, salty, buttery olive oil bath. To keep the sauce warm, use either a little fondue pot stand or something comparable outfitted with a candle or sterno. Otherwise, reheat the sauce over the stove as needed to keep it warm.

Put ½ cup (2 sticks) butter, ½ cup really good extra-virgin olive oil, 12 chopped anchovy filets, 1 minced garlic clove, juice of ½ lemon, and a little salt into a small heavy pot and gently warm over medium-low heat, stirring frequently, until the butter is melted and the anchovies have dissolved. Serve the sauce warm with sliced raw vegetables such as zucchini, cauliflower, celery, carrots, fennel, radishes, and bell peppers for dipping in at the table. —— *makes about 1 cup*

OUR BOOKS

This is the fourth book of our recipe collections—Canal House Cooking. We publish three seasonal volumes a year, each filled with delicious recipes for you from us. To sign up for a subscription or to buy books, visit thecanalhouse.com.

OUR WEBSITE

Our website, thecanalhouse.com, a companion to this book, offers our readers ways to get the best from supermarkets (what and how to buy, how to store it, cook it, and serve it). We'll tell you why a certain cut of meat works for a particular recipe, which boxes, cans, bottles, or tins are worthwhile; which apples are best for baking; and what to look for when buying olive oil, salt, or butter. We'll also suggest what's worth seeking out from specialty stores or mail-order sources and why. And wait, there's more. We share our stories, the wines we are drinking, gardening tips, and events; and our favorite books, cooks, and restaurants are on our site—take a look.